It's My Body

Body Pairs

Lola M. Schaefer

Heinemann Library
Chicago, Illinois

Customer Service 888-454-2279
Visit our website at www.heinemannlibrary.com

Designed by Sue Emerson, Heinemann Library; Page layout by Que-Net Media
Printed and bound in the United States by Lake Book Manufacturing, Inc.
Photo research by Jennifer Gillis

07 06 05 04 03
10 9 8 7 6 5 4 3 2 1

Library of Congress Cataloging-in-Publication Data
Schaefer, Lola M., 1950-
   Body pairs / Lola M. Schaefer.
        p. cm. – (It's my body)
Includes index.
Summary: Photographs and simple text depict, in increasing numbers, parts of the body that come in pairs, such as hands, thumbs, and knees.
   ISBN 1-4034-0895-5 (HC), 1-4034-3479-4 (Pbk.)
   1. Body, Human–Juvenile literature. 2. Counting--Juvenile literature. [1. Body, Human. 2. Counting.] I. Title.
II. Series:
Schaefer, Lola M., 1950-   . It's my body.
   QM27 .S367 2003
   611–dc21

                              2002014736

Acknowledgments
The author and publishers are grateful to the following for permission to reproduce copyright material:
pp. 3, 5, 7, 11 Brian Warling/Heinemann Library; pp. 9, 19, 21, 22 Robert Lifson/Heinemann Library; p. 13 Index Stock Imagery; pp. 15, 17 Bob Daemmrich/Stock Boston Inc./PictureQuest; p. 23 column 1 Brian Warling/Heinemann Library; Warling/Heinemann Library; column 2 (T-B) Robert Lifson/Heinemann Library, EyeWire/Getty Images; back cover (L-R) Brian Warling/Heinemann Library, Robert Lifson/Heinemann Library

Cover photographs (clockwise, starting top left) by Brian Warling/Heinemann Library, Robert Lifson/Heinemann Library, Robert Lifson/Heinemann Library

Every effort has been made to contact copyright holders of any material reproduced in this book. Any omissions will be rectified in subsequent printings if notice is given to the publisher.

Special thanks to our advisory panel for their help in the preparation of this book:

Alice Bethke, Library Consultant
Palo Alto, CA

Eileen Day, Preschool Teacher
Chicago, IL

Kathleen Gilbert,
Second Grade Teacher
Round Rock, TX

Sandra Gilbert,
Library Media Specialist
Fiest Elementary School
Houston, TX

Jan Gobeille,
Kindergarten Teacher
Garfield Elementary
Oakland, CA

Angela Leeper,
Educational Consultant
North Carolina Department
of Public Instruction
Wake Forest, NC

Some words are shown in bold, **like this.**
You can find them in the picture glossary on page 23.

What Is a Pair?

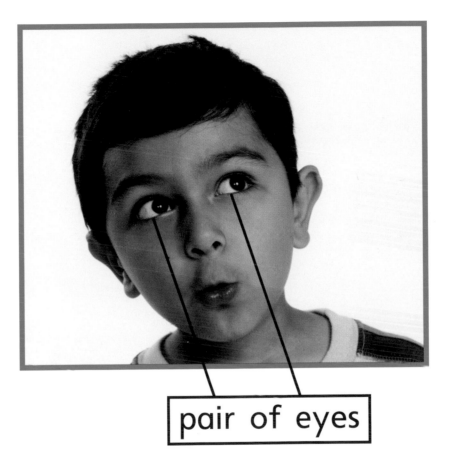

pair of eyes

Two things that look alike make a pair.

What parts of your body come in pairs?

One Pair 1

Your two hands look alike.

Your two hands make
one pair.

Two Pairs   2

Pairs of thumbs make spots on the ladybug.

How many pairs of thumbs do you see?

Three Pairs   3

Pairs of arms hang from the **monkey bars.**

How many pairs of arms do you see?

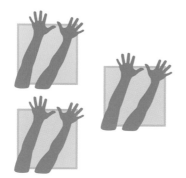

1 **2** **3**

Four Pairs 4

Pairs of **elbows** lean on the floor.

How many pairs of elbows do you see?

Five Pairs   5

Pairs of lips are smiling.

How many pairs of lips
do you see?

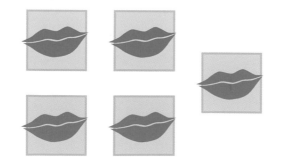

Six Pairs 6

Pairs of eyes watch
the **parade**.

How many pairs of eyes
do you see?

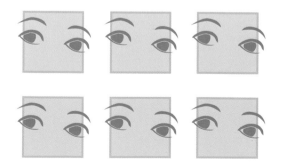

Seven Pairs 7

Pairs of legs are ready
to dance.

How many pairs of legs
do you see?

Eight Pairs   8

Pairs of **knees** bend.

How many pairs of knees
do you see?

Nine Pairs   9

Ankles join your feet to your legs.

How many pairs of ankles do you see?

How Many Pairs?

Pairs of feet stand in the grass.

How many pairs of feet do you see?

How many feet do you see
all together?

Look for the answers on page 24.

Picture Glossary

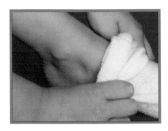 **ankle**
page 20

 **monkey bars**
page 8

 **elbow**
page 10

 **parade**
page 14

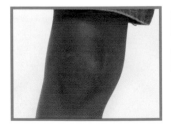 **knee**
page 18

Note to Parents and Teachers

This book familiarizes children with small sets of like things and the fact that, no matter where they are or what their size, a pair—a set of two—is always the same. You can help children practice this concept by randomly arranging an assortment of pairs, such as shoes, socks, mittens, earrings, and so on, on a table. Children can match up the pairs. Assist children in using the picture glossary and the index to practice new vocabulary and research skills.

Index

Answers to quiz on page 22

There are 10 pairs of feet.
There are 20 feet all together!

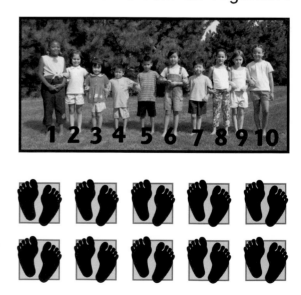

24